AF594800

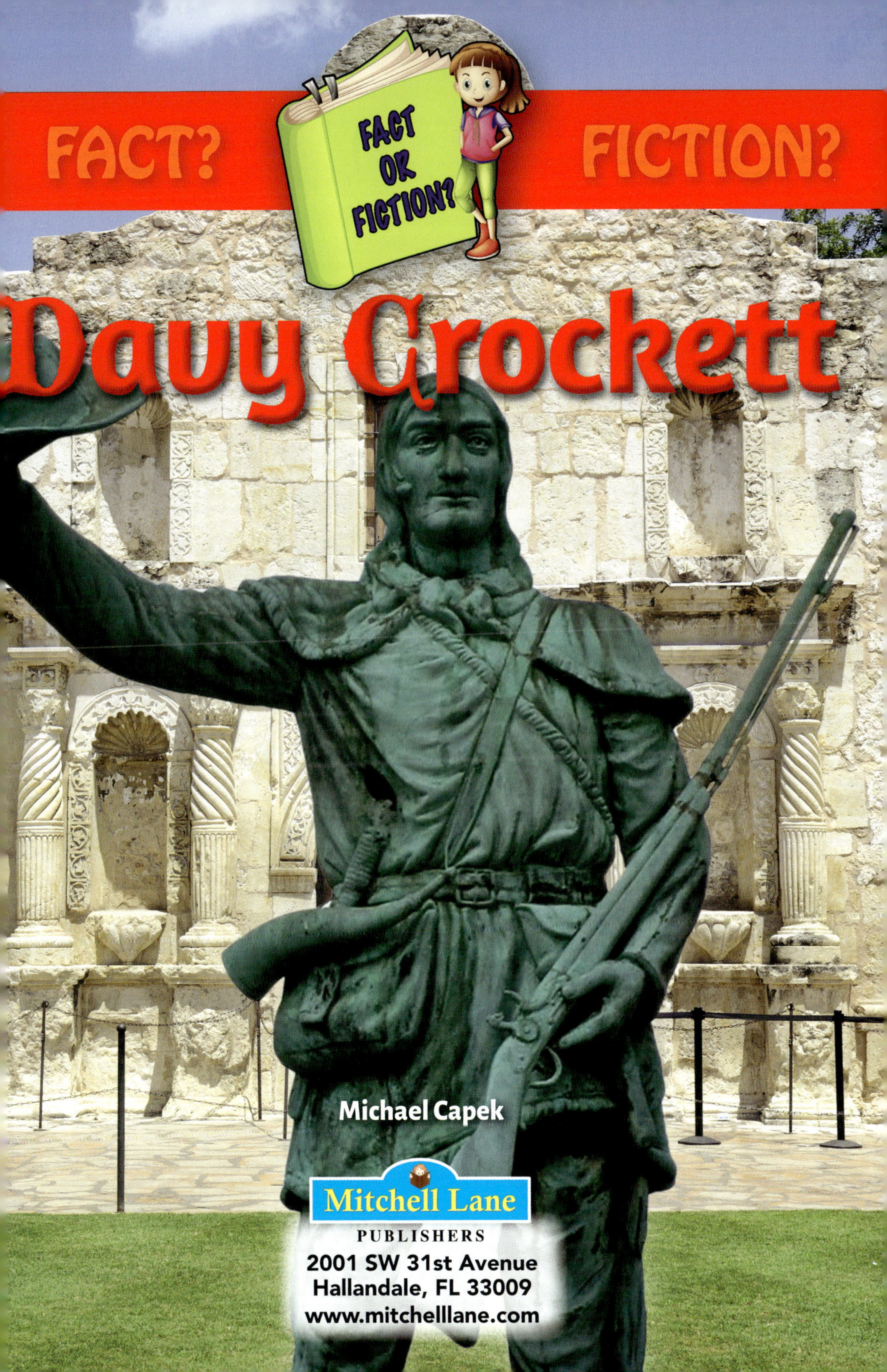

Davy Crockett

Michael Capek

Mitchell Lane
PUBLISHERS
2001 SW 31st Avenue
Hallandale, FL 33009
www.mitchelllane.com

Printing 1 2 3 4 5 6 7 8

Audie Murphy
Buffalo Bill Cody
The Buffalo Soldiers
Davy Crockett
Ethan Allen and the Green Mountain Boys
Eliot Ness
Francis Marion
The Pony Express
Robin Hood
The Tuskegee Airmen
Wyatt Earp
Zorro

Library of Congress Cataloging-in-Publication Data
Names: Capek, Michael, author.
Title: Davy Crockett / by Michael Capek.
Description: Hallandale, FL : Mitchell Lane Publishers, [2018] | Series: Fact or fiction? | Audience: Ages 8-11. | Audience: Grades 4-6.
Identifiers: LCCN 2017009120 | ISBN 9781612289748 (library bound)
Subjects: LCSH: Crockett, Davy, 1786–1836—Juvenile literature. | Pioneers—Tennessee—Biography—Juvenile literature. | Alamo (San Antonio, Tex.)—Siege, 1836—Juvenile literature.
Classification: LCC F436.C95 C35 2018 | DDC 976.804092 [B] —dc23
LC record available at https://lccn.loc.gov/2017009120

eBook ISBN: 978-1-61228-975-5

CONTENTS

Words in **bold** throughout can be found in the Glossary.

John Henry Huddle's portrait of Davy Crockett, decked out in his buckskin hunting clothes and carrying his rifle and coonskin cap, hangs in the Texas State Capitol Building in Austin. It's right next to another Huddle painting, "The Surrender of Santa Anna."

CHAPTER 1

Davy Learns to Grin

Who was Davy Crockett? Somebody once posed him that very question. Here's what he said: "I'm Davy Crockett. I'm half-horse, half-alligator, and a little touched with snapping turtle. I can wade the Mississippi, leap the Ohio, and ride on a streak of lightning. I can whip my weight in wildcats. If you throw in a ten dollar bill, I'll fight a bear and a panther, too."[1]

Another time he claimed he could run faster, jump higher, squat lower, dive deeper, stay underwater longer, and come up drier than any other man in the whole country.[2]

He even saved the world from disaster. That was in 1835, when Halley's Comet threatened to burn up the Earth. At least that's what simple folks thought was about to happen. Davy didn't wait to find out. He just reached up and twisted the tail right off of that old sparkler. Then he threw it back into space like a fiery snowball.[3]

That was Davy Crockett. Most people would say he was the talkingest, most rip-snorting, rough-and-readiest, fall-down-funniest critter they ever met. He had the most powerful bright grin they ever saw, they would add.

Some people say Davy saw his first light on a high mountaintop. Others say he started life in a valley near the Nolichucky River in eastern Tennessee. All that is known for sure is that he came into the world on August 17, 1786.

He was the youngest of nine children born to John and Rebecca Crockett. They were just poor dirt farmers and hunting was about the only way they could keep the kids fed and clothed. Davy helped out right from the start. He claimed he bagged his first bear when he was only three.

There's little question that Davy Crockett was born in Green County, Tennessee, in 1786. But did he really die at the Alamo in San Antonio, Texas, in 1836, as most history books say? David, the man, almost certainly did. Davy the legend, however, is still very much alive in the images and stories he helped create.

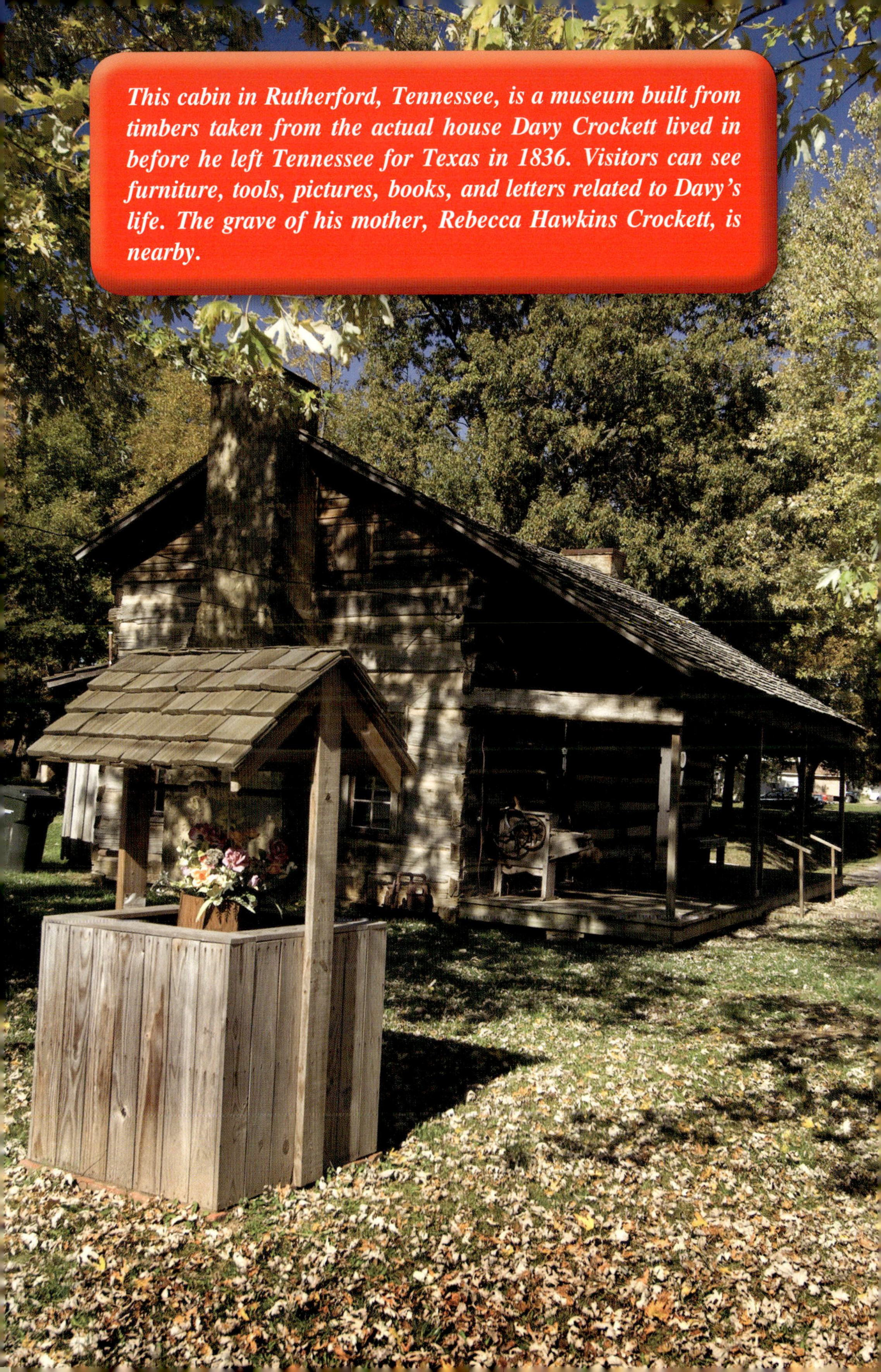

This cabin in Rutherford, Tennessee, is a museum built from timbers taken from the actual house Davy Crockett lived in before he left Tennessee for Texas in 1836. Visitors can see furniture, tools, pictures, books, and letters related to Davy's life. The grave of his mother, Rebecca Hawkins Crockett, is nearby.

According to his story, he was out in the woods, chewing on a giant oak tree. A hungry old bear came waddling out of a thicket. He took one look at Davy and his belly rumbled.

Roaring like a whirlwind, the beast charged. Davy heard the ruckus and turned. He gazed at the big furry beast, fascinated. He thought it was just a big, fuzzy toy.

The bear kept coming snapping and growling. When it got close, Davy stood up and grinned at it. He only had a few teeth, but it didn't matter. That grin flashed like a bolt of bright lightning. The bear took one look at it, whimpered like a kitten, and keeled over dead.[4]

After that, Davy kept his family well-supplied with meat. As he grew older, he also developed a taste for raccoon meat. He even took to wearing their fur as a hat, with the tail still attached. Grinning coons down was so easy that he never had to fire a shot.

Later on, Davy found that he favored his rifle, Betsy, more than his grin. In fact, Betsy was his first true love.[5]

One time, he lined up against some of the best sharpshooters in Tennessee in a contest. One of them was famous for his fancy shooting and his bragging. He had not heard of Davy. All he saw was this skinny kid in a coonskin cap. The man sneered. "Nobody in the world can out-shoot me!" he boasted. "Especially not some ignorant backwoods dandy wearing his dinner on his head."

The others realized it was Davy. They'd heard of his eagle eye and backed out of the contest.

Davy and the loud-mouthed stranger set up targets on two separate trees. They backed off a hundred paces and powdered their guns.

Davy's rival fired first. Both shots were inside the bullseye on his tree.

Now it was Davy's turn. His first ball hit the target on his tree dead center. But his next shot left no mark at all.

"You have missed the whole blamed target!" the big man roared, laughing in Davy's face.

Davy did not blink. "Let's go and have a look." Sure enough, on his target was only one round hole. The large man began to celebrate.

"Not so fast," Davy said. He pulled out his hunting knife and dug two bullets out of the same hole. The other man stopped dancing. He didn't look quite so smug now. He had to admit he had never seen such shooting in his life. After that, Davy's name and fame began to spread beyond the backwoods.[6]

Apparently Davy had pulled a fast one. His second shot had missed the target entirely. He decided to try to bluff the spectators. While no one was looking, he plucked a bullet out of his pocket and pushed it on top of his first shot. The ruse worked! "They were all perfectly satisfied, that fame had not made too great a flourish of trumpets when speaking of me as a marksman," he said.[7]

In 1834, near the end of Davy Crockett's political career (and his life), artist John Gadsby Chapman painted his portrait. It was stiff, formal, and solemn. Davy protested, so Gadsby started over. This cheerful portrait of Davy with his rifle and hunting dogs was Crockett's favorite image of himself. It was exactly how he wanted people to remember him.

CHAPTER 2
Bear Hunting

One of Davy's most famous legendary exploits didn't involve shooting. But like his first one, it did involve a bear. Davy loved nothing better than hunting bears. It's hard and dangerous. Bears are mean and particularly ferocious when they're cornered.

One day, Davy and his dogs tracked a bear all afternoon. He was big. Davy could see that from his tracks. It might even be the biggest bear in all of the forests of America, he figured. The creature was smart, too. It dodged and jittered like a shadow, looking for a good place to make his stand. He stayed out of sight and out of range until night fell.

In the icy chill of night, Davy's dogs followed the bear by scent. Near midnight, they cornered him.

Davy heard the dogs whooping and howling. When he got to where they were, all he could see in the darkness were black shapes moving about. He called back the dogs. Strangely, he heard the bear snarling below his feet. Davy felt the ground and found that the bear was in a natural crack, or **crevice**, in the rocky ground. The beast had the upper hand for sure. But Davy wasn't going to let him get away.

During the 19th century, hand-colored illustrations like this one appeared in publications such as the Davy Crockett Almanack. *Stories and pictures in the books were often wildly exaggerated versions of the truth. They sought more to entertain readers rather than inform them about real events and people.*

Betsy was no good in the dark. He tossed her aside and pulled out his foot-long hunting knife. Then he lowered himself into the narrow opening.

The bear smelled him. He roared, a blast of stinking breath that blew Davy's coonskin cap plumb off. The monster lunged, trying to grab Davy and hug him to death, as bears will. Davy dodged the razor claws and dagger teeth.

The dogs sensed Davy was in danger. They rushed to the hole and jumped in, biting and snapping. The bear turned away from Davy to face them. That was the opening Davy needed. He reached out with his left hand and felt the bear's rump. Sliding his hand up, he searched for the creature's shoulder. As soon as he touched it, he jabbed with all his might. The blade found the bear's heart on the first try. It gave a roar heard clear in the next county before it fell over dead.[1]

This knife, on display in the San Jacinto Museum of History in Houston, Texas, is said to have been used by Davy Crockett during his final days. According to museum records, it was picked up after Crockett's death at the Alamo by a woman who witnessed the battle.

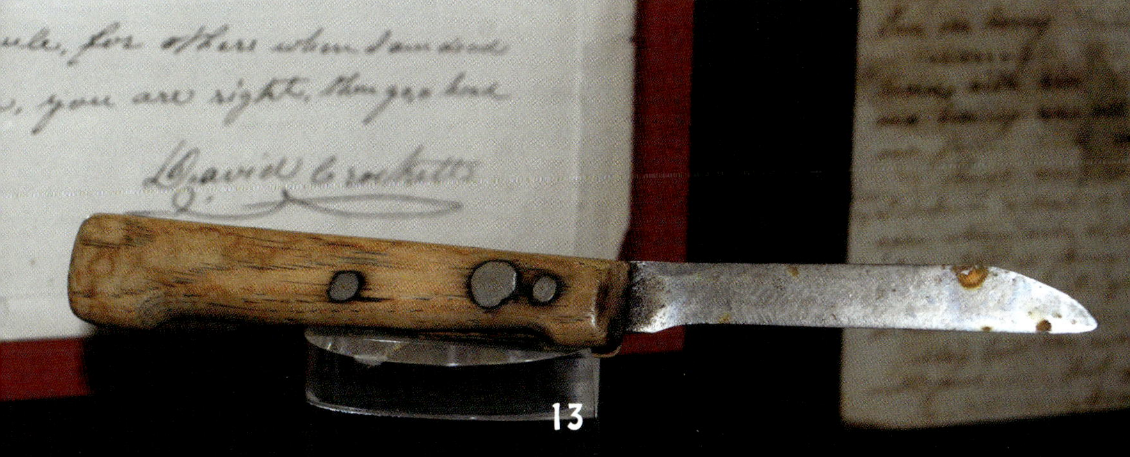

"Be sure you are right, then go ahead." Crockett's now-famous words are etched in granite on the 13-foot-tall monument located in the Orzona, Texas city park. The bas-relief figure by artist William Mozart McVey was dedicated in 1939. Orzona, like at least a dozen other cities, hosts a Davy Crockett Festival every year.

CHAPTER 3

"Always Be Sure You Are Right"

In 1812, war broke out between the United States and the British. About that time, Davy got a powerful itch to move west. By now he was married and had three children. East Tennessee was filling up with new settlers. Things were getting crowded. Game was harder to find. Besides, Davy always craved elbow room.

He settled in Franklin County, Tennessee, about ten miles from the Alabama border.[1] This land had been home to the Creek Indians for centuries. They did not take kindly to strangers settling and hunting on their land. Davy never had anything against the Indians, and he always got along with folks. He only took what he needed from the woods. The Creeks left him alone.

That changed when the British stirred up the Indians against the settlers. The Indians began by attacking forts. Davy figured that was fine. Warriors against soldiers was a fair fight. But then Indians began to burn towns and settlers' homes. Davy knew his family was in danger. Other settlers in the area formed a **militia**, and Davy joined up as a scout. The men decided to help the American army. Davy was

President Andrew Jackson and Davy Crockett were both Tennessee natives. But they didn't agree on several important political issues. When Congressman Crockett openly stated his opinions, Jackson made sure Davy was not re-elected.

happy when he heard that General Andrew Jackson, a Tennessee man nicknamed "Old Hickory," led the army.

Davy's ability to track in deep woods helped the army find the Indians. His talent for hunting kept the soldiers fed. Davy was an able fighter, too. He and his men fought in battles with the soldiers against the Creek Indians. Davy showed his natural gift for leadership and quick thinking under fire.

But Davy never could get used to killing other people. Even if the Indians were the enemy, Davy felt deep down that they were only doing what he would do in their place. Weren't they just protecting their homes and families, too?[2]

One day, Davy was out scouting with his friend, George Russell. They came upon a large group of Creek warriors camped in a clearing. George wanted to go back and get reinforcements, but Davy stopped him. "There'll just be another battle, and a whole passel of people will get killed. I've got a better idea. Let's give them the

Crockett charge." He told George what to do, and the men separated.

In a few minutes, the Indians were startled to hear gunshots all around them. Someone in the woods to their right yelled, "Company A! Prepare to attack!" Moments later, on their left, another voice shouted. "Company B! Get ready to charge!" Behind them, they heard still more shooting and the sounds of officers moving even more soldiers into position. Sure that they were surrounded, the Creeks threw down their weapons and gave up. To their utter amazement, only two men appeared. One was Davy, grinning like a possum. Soon after, soldiers arrived and took the warriors as prisoners. Davy was pleased as punch. At least for one day, nobody died.[3]

The minute his volunteer time was up, Davy wanted to go home. But Andrew Jackson decided he wasn't quite finished with Davy and his men. He ordered them to stay. When Davy said they were going anyway, Jackson ordered soldiers to block the only road out of camp. He even placed a cannon there. "Shoot the first man who tries to leave!" he shouted. Davy just grinned and calmly led his men past the soldiers and out of camp. Davy knew Jackson would never shoot militiamen from his own state.[4]

Somebody asked Davy later how he had the courage to face down Andrew Jackson. "I knew I was right," he said. After that, a certain saying became part of Davy's way of talking and thinking: "Always be sure you are right. Then go ahead." That motto guided him for the rest of his life.[5]

This 1834 portrait by artist Chester Harding has been described as perhaps the most accurate picture made of "The Canebreak Congressman," yet another of Davy's many nicknames. Crockett himself thought it made him look too much "like a Methodist preacher." The painting is now in the National Portrait Gallery in Washington, D.C.

CHAPTER 4

The Lion of the West

After the Creek War ended, Davy's name and fame kept getting bigger and bigger. He kept moving west, too. The **frontier** was always where he wanted to be. But people had a way of pulling him back to civilization by electing him to public office.

Davy started out as a local **magistrate**. He was a fair, impartial judge. That led to other, bigger elections and more important duties. Settlers in the backwoods needed somebody to stand up for them in the Tennessee state **legislature**. In 1821, they elected Davy to do that.

It turned out he was a natural **politician**. He did such a good job representing poor and common folks that they sent him to Washington, D.C. six years later. He served in the U.S. Congress for three two-year terms.

Davy had become a regular folk hero. Books and **almanacs** popped up everywhere. Stories about his daring deeds and adventures appeared in newspapers. He even wrote a book about his life. For somebody with only a few months of schooling, that's a spectacular feat all by itself.

A play called *The Lion of the West* came out in 1831. The main character was a rip-snorting backwoodsman called Colonel Nimrod Wildfire. Everybody knew who Wildfire was supposed to be. He talked like Davy and even dressed in animal skins. Davy went to see the play one night. When the actor playing Wildfire came on stage, he bowed to Davy. Davy stood and bowed back. The crowd stomped, whistled, and cheered. Davy lapped it up like gravy. He began making public appearances dressed in his

A cartoon that appeared around 1832 shows a backwoods politician, supposedly Davy Crockett, campaigning for office. He's giving one voter a drink and another some tobacco. Such shady practices were commonplace, and even expected, in rural areas in the early 19th century.

old hunting clothes and raccoon hat. His popularity soared. People loved Davy's honest, funny, homespun style. And if there was one thing, other than hunting, that Davy knew how to do, it was talking.

Some people called him "the most popular son Tennessee ever produced." For a while, there was serious talk that Davy was on his way to the White House. But someone else from Tennessee was already there. It was Andrew Jackson.

Davy and President Jackson were on different sides of the political fence. Davy figured that Old Hickory wasn't doing right by poor folks. He also didn't like the way Jackson wanted to just sweep the Indians off the map. Davy always believed Indians deserved their own homes and said so in speech after speech. But this time, nobody was listening.

President Jackson was too powerful. In the end, he got his way. The Indians lost their longtime homelands and Davy lost his seat in Congress in 1835.[1]

His political career was finished, but his legend wasn't.

Mexican president and general Antonio López de Santa Anna led the army that defeated the defenders of the Alamo in March, 1836. A month later, his troops were beaten at the Battle of San Jacinto. He was forced to sign a treaty giving Texas its independence. Santa Anna returned to Mexico in disgrace, but soon after was reelected president. He served in that office for eleven terms that spanned 22 years.

CHAPTER 5
Gone to Texas

In November 1835, Davy announced he was moving west. He'd heard about Texas, where people were fighting for their **independence** from Mexico. Davy had gotten his fill of soldiering during the Creek War. He didn't want any more. Still, people were fighting for their freedom. He couldn't stay away.

As soon as he saw Texas, he fell in love. It was beautiful country, filled with wild game and sweeping scenery. He could not wait to bring his family there.

But first, he had to help make it safe for settlers and their families. He signed a **loyalty oath**. It was a promise that he'd support and fight for Texas anyplace he was needed. At the moment, that place looked like the Alamo, the little mission-turned-fort near the San Antonio River where a small group of freedom fighters was holed up. Two officers, William Travis and James Bowie, led the volunteers inside the Alamo. They had gone there determined to stop an army moving north from Mexico. General Antonio López de Santa Anna, a proud and brutal warrior, led that force. Texas still belonged to Mexico, and Santa Anna wanted to make a point. He'd crush the little band of fighters at the Alamo. That would show other rebels they had no chance of ever making Texas into a **republic**.

It was clear that the volunteers at the Alamo were in terrible danger. They had little hope against an army of thousands of Mexican soldiers.

Davy made a beeline to the Alamo anyway. He arrived in February, 1836, just ahead of Santa Anna. Quickly, the Mexican force surrounded the fortress and sent word for the rebels to surrender. The Texans answered with a blast from a cannon. The Mexicans opened fire with cannon blasts of their own. Inside the fort, Davy and the other defenders hunkered down. Things looked mighty dark.

The Alamo was a small Spanish mission when it was manned as a fort by Mexican soldiers in 1835. They were driven out by a force of Texans. Santa Anna soon recaptured it. The ruined fort and its fallen defenders became symbols in the continuing fight for Texas independence. "Remember the Alamo!" became an American rallying cry ever after.

Davy tried to raise the men's spirits. He joked and told tall tales that made the men laugh. He seemed so confident, they began to feel better.

The Mexican soldiers in their blue uniforms attacked. Cannon shells rained down on the little fort. Soldiers charged the flimsy front gate and tried to break it down. Others tried to scale the walls using log ladders. Time after time, Davy and his sharpshooters pushed them back.

For 10 days, the fighting went on. Again and again, the Mexican soldiers charged the Alamo, fell back, and charged again. The Texas fighters killed hundreds. But Santa Anna would not stop. The brave men inside the Alamo were beaten and hungry. Some were wounded and dying.

Before dawn on March 5, Travis and Bowie called everyone together. Travis drew a line in the sand. "Whoever wants to stay and fight, step across the line now. Those who've had enough are welcome to leave. No one will call you a coward." With one exception, every man crossed the line.[1]

Early the next morning, thousands of Mexican soldiers charged the Alamo. Almost immediately, the Texans ran out of bullets and gunpowder. Hundreds of Mexicans broke down the gate and poured inside. Hundreds more swarmed over the walls. Davy and the others used knives, swords, clubs, and anything else they could find to fight with. Davy could not stand to part with old Betsy, even if he had nothing left to load her with. He grasped the rifle by the barrel and swung it like a club.

The image of Davy Crockett the hero standing firm, fighting to the death against a host of Mexican attackers as the Alamo fell, is one of the most enduring and stirring parts of his legend. The historical facts, however, have become blurred over the years by a multitude of popular books and movies.

After a time, Davy looked around. Nearly all the wall defenders were gone now, either dead or wounded. The yard below was swarming with Mexican soldiers. They were slashing and firing at the few remaining Texans who had gathered near the church at the back of the Alamo.

Davy turned away. There was nothing left to do now but keep fighting. He began to swing his broken rifle at any blue coat he could reach. The last thing many men saw that day was Davy Crockett bravely swinging Betsy over his head.

The Alamo Cenotaph (empty tomb) on the Alamo Plaza in San Antonio, Texas, is 60 feet high. Titled "the Spirit of Sacrifice," the granite monument is the work of artist Pompeo Coppini. It was dedicated in 1940 to the memory of the fallen defenders of the Alamo. The representative figures carved on its base include Davy Crockett (holding his rifle Betsy).

FACT OR FICTION?

Tales of David and Davy

Born on a mountaintop in Tennessee,
Greenest state in the land of the free,
Raised in the woods so he knew every tree,
Kilt him a b'ar when he was only three.
Davy, Davy Crockett, King of the wild frontier![1]

Much of what people think they know about Davy Crockett comes from a 1954 Walt Disney television series called *Davy Crockett*. The following year, Disney released the movie *Davy Crockett: King of the Wild Frontier*, which included this rousing song. Americans went Crockett-crazy. Stores sold millions of Crockett toys, lunchboxes, books, and clothes. Every kid wanted a coonskin cap.[2] The fad died down quickly. But another movie, *The Alamo*, brought it back in 1960. John Wayne, a national hero himself, played Davy.

The legend began many years earlier. Long before Disney or John Wayne, David Crockett was a smash hit who started his own legend. That's what he liked to call himself—David, not Davy. He discovered at a young age that he had a special gift for making people laugh. Telling tall tales was something many people did in early America. David had a real flair for it. He told many stories about himself during his political campaigns. Many were clearly made up and some were just plain silly. People didn't care. David's honest grin and easygoing backwoods style got him elected again and again. In the 1830s, newspapers and magazines rewrote these stories. They made David Crockett famous. He became a superstar.

In 1834, he published *A Narrative of the Life of David Crockett*. It contains many of the stories he'd been telling for years, along with a few facts. He said the book presented "the exact image of its author."[3] In David's case, the image he wanted to present was Davy, the legend.

The Lion of the West also helped create the "Davy Legend." So did a series of magazines published between 1835 and 1856 called the *Crockett Almanacs*. Almanacs contained useful information for farmers and homeowners. They also had stories and tall tales based on real and imaginary frontier heroes. Many of them, such as the Halley's Comet story, made him seem almost superhuman, like Paul Bunyan. Tales far weirder continued to add to Davy Crockett's legend even after his death.[4]

In most cases, it's easy to tell the difference between fact and fiction in the Davy legends. There are two different stories—tales of David, the man, and Davy, the legend.

Things that make him appear superhuman are part of the Davy legend. Other things, even those such as his hunting adventures and war stories that seem hard to believe, may actually be true.

David was certainly a war hero and a noted frontiersman. His time as a scout and fighter in the Creek Indian War is part of the historical record. So is his role in surveying and opening the backwoods of Tennessee for settlers. Even the story about Davy's killing a cornered bear using only his knife probably did happen. Historians believe he might well have killed (or helped kill) 105 bears in one season, as well.[5]

David Crockett's political career is very real, too. He did care a great deal about the poor and Native Americans. Andrew Jackson clearly did not.[6] David spent a great deal of time and effort trying to get bills passed in Congress to help them. He even thought seriously about running for president. But David was never quite as good at politics as he was at getting elected. He never could convince others in power to support his ideas. In the end, he grew tired of the bickering and bargaining in Washington. He was disappointed when he wasn't re-elected in 1835. But he must have been relieved, too. He was clearly excited about going to Texas and starting over.[7]

The Alamo story above is based mostly on the Disney movie and popular tradition. David didn't go to Texas just to fight for freedom. He did fall in love with Texas. That much is true. He did sign the pledge of allegiance and agreed to fight. He still did not have to go to the Alamo, though. He chose to do that on his own.

Until recently, nearly everyone thought David died fighting, swinging Betsy like a baseball bat. But newer evidence suggests that he may have been captured early in the morning of that last day. An eyewitness reported that David was taken prisoner. He was executed with the handful of other captives soon afterward.[8]

In spite of the evidence, many people do not want to believe that David surrendered willingly. "Davy would never give up," they insist. And they're right. Davy, the legend, never would. But David, the real man, might have. He had a great deal to live for, after all. He was only 49 years old. And maybe he thought he could grin and talk his way out of trouble. Or perhaps he thought his name and fame might save him. If so, sadly, he was wrong.

So, David died that day. But Davy lives on. Both are still worth remembering.

CHAPTER NOTES

Chapter 1: Davy Learns to Grin

1. *Sketches and Eccentricities of Col. David Crockett of West Tennessee*. New York: J. & J. Harper, 1833, p. 164.
2. Michael Lofaro, *The Tall Tales of Davy Crockett: The Second Nashville Series of Crockett Almanacs, 1839–1841* (Knoxville, TN: University of Tennessee Press, 1987), p. xxvi.
3. Ibid., p. 26.
4. *Sketches and Eccentricities*, p. 164.
5. David Crockett, *A Narrative of the Life of David Crockett of the State of Tennessee* (Lincoln, NE: University of Nebraska Press, 1987), p. 50.
6. "Target Shooting," *The Life of David Crockett* (1860). http://xroads.virginia.edu/~HYPER/DETOC/sw/crockett1.html
7. Ibid.

Chapter 2: Bear Hunting

1. David Crockett, *A Narrative of the Life of David Crockett of the State of Tennessee* (Lincoln, NE: University of Nebraska Press, 1987), pp. 188–90.

Chapter 3: "Always Be Sure You Are Right"

1. James A. Shackford, *David Crockett: The Man and the Legend* (Chapel Hill, NC: University of North Carolina Press, 1986), p. 18.
2. Buddy Levy, *American Legend: The Real-Life Adventures of David Crockett* (New York: G.P. Putnam's Sons, 2005), pp. 167–68.
3. Norman Foster, director. *Walt Disney Treasures: Davy Crockett—The Complete Television Series*. Walt Disney Video, 2001.
4. David Crockett, *A Narrative of the Life of David Crockett of the State of Tennessee* (Lincoln, NE: University of Nebraska Press, 1987), pp. 93–95.
5. Shackford, pp. 26, 136.

Chapter 4: The Lion of the West

1. Buddy Levy, *American Legend: The Real-Life Adventures of David Crockett* (New York: G.P. Putnam's Sons, 2005), pp. 168–70.

Chapter 5: Gone to Texas

1. "13 Days of Glory," The Alamo: The Shrine of Texas Liberty. http://www.thealamo.org/history/the-1836-battle/13-days.html

Fact or Fiction: The Tales of David and Davy

1. "Davy Crockett, Tall Tales, and History: Introduction," National Endowment for the Humanities. http://edsitement.neh.gov/lesson-plan/davy-crockett-tall-tales-and-history
2. Bob Thompson, *Born On a Mountaintop: On the Road with Davy Crockett and the Ghosts of the Wild Frontier* (New York: Crown Trade Group, 2012), pp. 248–49.
3. David Crockett, *A Narrative of the Life of David Crockett of the State of Tennessee* (Lincoln, NE: University of Nebraska Press, 1987), p. 11.
4. "Davy Crockett, 1786-1836," Know Southern History. http://www.knowsouthernhistory.net/Biographies/Davy_Crockett/
5. James A. Shackford, *David Crockett: The Man and the Legend* (Chapel Hill, NC: University of North Carolina Press, 1986), p. 63.
6. Buddy Levy, *American Legend: The Real-Life Adventures of David Crockett* (New York: G.P. Putnam's Sons, 2005), p. 166.
7. Ibid., p. 247.
8. "David (Davy) Crockett," The Alamo: The Shrine of Texas Liberty. http://www.thealamo.org/history/the-1836-battle/the-defenders/defenders/crockett.html

PHOTO CREDITS: All design elements from Thinkstock/Sharon Beck; Cover, p. 1—robertcicchetti/Getty Images Plus; p. 4—William Henry Huddle/Dallas Museum of Art, The Karl and Esther Hoblitzelle Collection, gift of the Hoblitzelle Foundation; p. 6—GDFL/cc by-sa 3.0; p. 7—Don Smetzer/Alamy Stock Photo; pp. 10, 20, 24—Library of Congress; p. 12—North Wind Picture Archives/Alamy Stock Photo; p. 13—Brian Reading/cc by-sa 3.0; p. 14—Brian Reading/Stephen Saks Photography/Alamy Stock Photo; p. 16—Thomas Sully/The Historical Society of Pennsylvania/Public domain; p. 18—Ian G Dagnall/Alamy Stock Photo; p. 22—World History Archive/Alamy Stock Photo; p. 26—ClassicStock/Alamy Stock Photo; p. 27—Alex Stork/Getty Images Plus

almanacs (ALL-muh-nacks)—books that contain interesting and useful information about the weather along with household and farming ideas
crevice (CREH-vuhss)—a crack or opening in the earth
frontier (fruhn-TIER)—land or area that is not yet settled
independence (in-dee-PEN-dense)—freedom from control by others
legislature (LEDGE-iss-lay-chur)—government branch consisting of people elected to make laws and take care of other public business
loyalty oath (LOYL-tee OATH)—agreement to support and defend a place or group of people
magistrate (MAJ-iss-trait)—a kind of judge
militia (muh-LISH-uh)—a group of volunteer citizens who become a fighting force
politician (pol-uh-TISH-un)—someone who takes part in government
republic (ree-PUB-lick)—a free state

WORKS CONSULTED

"13 Days of Glory." The Alamo: The Shrine of Texas Liberty. http://www.thealamo.org/history/the-1836-battle/13-days.html

Crockett, David. *A Narrative of the Life of David Crockett of the State of Tennessee*. Lincoln, NE: University of Nebraska Press, 1987.

"David (Davy) Crockett." The Alamo: The Shrine of Texas Liberty. http://www.thealamo.org/history/the-1836-battle/the-defenders/defenders/crockett.html

"Davy Crockett, 1786-1836." Know Southern History. http://www.knowsouthernhistory.net/Biographies/Davy_Crockett/

"Davy Crockett, Tall Tales, and History: Introduction." National Endowment for the Humanities. http://edsitement.neh.gov/lesson-plan/davy-crockett-tall-tales-and-history

Foster, Norman. *Walt Disney Treasures: Davy Crockett—The Complete Television Series*. Walt Disney Video, 2001.

Levy, Buddy. *American Legend: The Real-Life Adventures of David Crockett*. New York: G.P. Putnam's Sons, 2005.

Lofaro, Michael. *The Tall Tales of Davy Crockett: The Second Nashville Series of Crockett Almanacs, 1839–1841*. Knoxville, TN: University of Tennessee Press, 1987.

Shackford, James A. *David Crockett: The Man and the Legend*. Chapel Hill, NC: University of North Carolina Press, 1986.

Sketches and Eccentricities of Col. David Crockett of West Tennessee. New York: J. & J. Harper, 1833.

"Target Shooting." *The Life of David Crockett* (1860). http://xroads.virginia.edu/~HYPER/DETOC/sw/crockett1.html

Thompson, Bob. *Born On a Mountaintop: On the Road with Davy Crockett and the Ghosts of the Wild Frontier*. New York: Crown Trade Group, 2012.

FURTHER READING

Belviso, Meg and Pamela Pollack. *What Was the Alamo?* New York: Grosset & Dunlap, 2013.

Herman, Gail. *Who Was Davy Crockett?* New York: Grosset & Dunlap, 2013.

Sanford, William and Carl Green. *Davy Crockett: Courageous Hero of the Alamo*. Berkeley Heights, NJ: Enslow, 2013.

Schanzer, Rosalyn. *Davy Crockett Saves the World*. New York: HarperCollins, 2001.

Sullivan, George. *Davy Crockett*. New York: Scholastic Press, 2001.

Winders, Richard B. *Davy Crockett: The Legend of the Wild Frontier*. New York: Rosen Publishing, 2003.

INDEX

ABOUT THE AUTHOR

Michael has been fascinated with Davy Crockett ever since he saw the original three-part series on the Walt Disney TV show in 1954. Like millions of other kids, he got a coonskin cap and plastic flintlock rifle and went ripping around the neighborhood singing "Davy! Davy Crockett! King of the Wild Frontier!" at the top of his lungs. Michael has always loved history. That interest has led to a lifetime of teaching, reading, and writing. He's the author of many nonfiction books (most of them about history) and a historical novel for young readers. Michael lives in northern Kentucky.